All rights reserved.
This publication is designed to provide information & enjoyment only.
It is sold with the understanding that the publisher and author is not engaged in rendering psychological, financial, legal or other professional services. Neither the publisher nor the author is engaged in rendering professional services or advice.
For more information contact moreenthetherapist@gmail.com

Copyright 2022 Moreen Jordan, M.A., L.P.C.
moreenjordan.com

The ideas, procedures, and suggestions contained in this book are not intended as a substitute for consulting with your physician or other health care provider. All matters regarding your health require medical supervision. Neither the author nor the publisher shall be liable for responsible for any loss or damages allegedly arising from any information or suggestion in this book.
If expert assistance or counseling is needed, the services of a competent professional should be sought.
All handouts and worksheets can be photocopied for personal use with this program, but may not be reproduced for any other purpose without the written permission of the copyright owner

ISBN: (paperback)

Printed in the United States of American

First Edition 2021
First Printing 2021

Welcome & Thank you

Congratulations

Self Care is important and you have taken a step forward by purchasing this workbook. I commend you for understanding how important your well being is. You have made yourself a priority. Doing so not only benefits you, but the people you love as well. The peopple who love you and depnd on you would much rather see you positive, full of energy and happy, than tired, unhappy and emotionally drainged.

This self care workbook will help to equip you with the knowledge and tools to make self care an ongoing part of your life's journey.

Thank you for choosing our workbook to assist you with your journey

Moreen Jordan, M.A., L.P.C.
Marital & Family Therapist

WHY I DESIRE IT- SELF-CARE

UNIVERSE BRINGS YOUR MANIFESTATIONS TO YOUR PHYSICAL TIMELINE MUCH FASTER IF YOU KNOW WHY EXACTLY YOU DESIRE WHAT YOU DESIRE. WRITE OUT WHY YOU WANT IT, WHERE YOU WANT TO UTILISE IT, ON WHOM YOU'RE GOING TO IMPLEMENT IT.
(DON'T FORGET YOURSELF & ALSO GIVING BACK TO OTHERS)

LET'S VISUALIZE IT! -- SELF-CARE

PUT YOUR ROSE-COLOURED GLASSES ON, AND VISUALIZE EVERY ASPECT OF MONEY & WEALTH YOU DESIRE TO MANIFEST INTO YOUR PHYSICAL REALITY. THINK OF THE TINIEST DETAILS. TOUCH EVERY SENSE OF MONEY. WHAT IT MEANS TO YOU, HOW YOU FEEL ABOUT IT & EVERY LITTLE DETAIL! PUT NO BOUNDARIES TO YOUR DESIRES, LET YOUR IMAGINATION RUN FREE & WILD!

what's coming is better than what's gone

THE 5-MINUTE JOURNAL

---START OF THE DAY---

NAME :   DATE: /   /

I AM GRATEFUL FOR ...

_____
_____
_____
_____

THINGS THAT WOULD MAKE TODAY GREAT...

_____
_____
_____
_____

DAILY AFFIRMATIONS . I AM...

_____
_____
_____
_____

THE 5-MINUTE JOURNAL

---START OF THE DAY---

NAME : DATE: / /

I AM GRATEFUL FOR ...

_____

_____

_____

THINGS THAT WOULD MAKE TODAY GREAT...

_____

_____

_____

DAILY AFFIRMATIONS . I AM...

_____

_____

_____

THE 5-MINUTE JOURNAL

---START OF THE DAY---

NAME : DATE: / /

I AM GRATEFUL FOR ...

_____

_____

_____

_____

_____

THINGS THAT WOULD MAKE TODAY GREAT...

_____

_____

_____

_____

_____

DAILY AFFIRMATIONS . I AM...

_____

_____

_____

_____

_____

THE 5-MINUTE JOURNAL

---START OF THE DAY---

NAME :   DATE: /   /

I AM GRATEFUL FOR ...

_____
_____
_____
_____

THINGS THAT WOULD MAKE TODAY GREAT...

_____
_____
_____
_____

DAILY AFFIRMATIONS . I AM...

_____
_____
_____
_____

THE 5-MINUTE JOURNAL

---START OF THE DAY---

NAME : DATE: / /

I AM GRATEFUL FOR ...

_____
_____
_____
_____

THINGS THAT WOULD MAKE TODAY GREAT...

_____
_____
_____

DAILY AFFIRMATIONS . I AM...

_____
_____
_____
_____

THE 5-MINUTE JOURNAL

---START OF THE DAY---

NAME : DATE: / /

I AM GRATEFUL FOR ...

_____
_____
_____
_____

THINGS THAT WOULD MAKE TODAY GREAT...

_____
_____
_____
_____

DAILY AFFIRMATIONS . I AM...

_____
_____
_____
_____

THE 5-MINUTE JOURNAL

---START OF THE DAY---

NAME :   DATE: /   /

I AM GRATEFUL FOR ...

_____

_____

_____

_____

THINGS THAT WOULD MAKE TODAY GREAT...

_____

_____

_____

_____

DAILY AFFIRMATIONS . I AM...

_____

_____

_____

_____

THE 5-MINUTE JOURNAL

---START OF THE DAY---

NAME : DATE: / /

I AM GRATEFUL FOR ...

_____
_____
_____
_____

THINGS THAT WOULD MAKE TODAY GREAT...

_____
_____
_____
_____

DAILY AFFIRMATIONS . I AM...

_____
_____
_____
_____

THE 5-MINUTE JOURNAL

---START OF THE DAY---

NAME :   DATE: /   /

I AM GRATEFUL FOR ...

_____
_____
_____
_____

THINGS THAT WOULD MAKE TODAY GREAT...

_____
_____
_____
_____

DAILY AFFIRMATIONS . I AM...

_____
_____
_____
_____

THE 5-MINUTE JOURNAL

---START OF THE DAY---

NAME : DATE: / /

I AM GRATEFUL FOR ...

_____
_____
_____
_____

THINGS THAT WOULD MAKE TODAY GREAT...

_____
_____
_____
_____

DAILY AFFIRMATIONS . I AM...

_____
_____
_____
_____

THE 5-MINUTE JOURNAL

---START OF THE DAY---

NAME : DATE: / /

I AM GRATEFUL FOR ...

_____
_____
_____
_____
_____

THINGS THAT WOULD MAKE TODAY GREAT...

_____
_____
_____
_____

DAILY AFFIRMATIONS . I AM...

_____
_____
_____
_____

WHY I DESIRE IT- HEALTH

UNIVERSE BRINGS YOUR MANIFESTATIONS TO YOUR PHYSICAL TIMELINE MUCH FASTER IF YOU KNOW WHY EXACTLY YOU DESIRE WHAT YOU DESIRE. WRITE OUT WHY YOU WANT IT, WHERE YOU WANT TO UTILISE IT, ON WHOM YOU'RE GOING TO IMPLEMENT IT.
(DON'T FORGET YOURSELF & ALSO GIVING BACK TO OTHERS)

HEALTH VISION BOARD

LET'S VISUALIZE IT! -- HEALTH

PUT YOUR ROSE-COLOURED GLASSES ON, AND VISUALIZE EVERY ASPECT OF MONEY & WEALTH YOU DESIRE TO MANIFEST INTO YOUR PHYSICAL REALITY. THINK OF THE TINIEST DETAILS. TOUCH EVERY SENSE OF MONEY. WHAT IT MEANS TO YOU, HOW YOU FEEL ABOUT IT & EVERY LITTLE DETAIL! PUT NO BOUNDARIES TO YOUR DESIRES, LET YOUR IMAGINATION RUN FREE & WILD!

LOVE VISION BOARD

My Partner

DESCRIBE THE TYPE OF ROMANTIC PARTNER YOU WANT TO ATTRACT.

Greatest possible thing you desire in terms of love

LOVE AFFIRMATIONS

1. I am open and ready to give and receive love.
2. I deserve a profoundly nurturing and fulfilling passion.
3. I am worthy of love.
4. I love myself.
5. I accept myself how I am and cultivate self-love.
6. I trust that love will find me.
7. True love starts within.
8. My heart offers love to all beings everywhere.
9. I am attracting a real connection.
10. I am loved and cherished by friends, family, and loved ones.

WHY I DESIRE IT- LOVE

UNIVERSE BRINGS YOUR MANIFESTATIONS TO YOUR PHYSICAL TIMELINE MUCH FASTER IF YOU KNOW WHY EXACTLY YOU DESIRE WHAT YOU DESIRE. WRITE OUT WHY YOU WANT IT, WHERE YOU WANT TO UTILISE IT, ON WHOM YOU'RE GOING TO IMPLEMENT IT.
(DON'T FORGET YOURSELF & ALSO GIVING BACK TO OTHERS)

LET'S VISUALIZE IT! -- LOVE

PUT YOUR ROSE-COLOURED GLASSES ON, AND VISUALIZE EVERY ASPECT OF MONEY & WEALTH YOU DESIRE TO MANIFEST INTO YOUR PHYSICAL REALITY. THINK OF THE TINIEST DETAILS. TOUCH EVERY SENSE OF MONEY. WHAT IT MEANS TO YOU, HOW YOU FEEL ABOUT IT & EVERY LITTLE DETAIL! PUT NO BOUNDARIES TO YOUR DESIRES, LET YOUR IMAGINATION RUN FREE & WILD!

CAREER VISION BOARD

I AM CREATING A LIFE OF MY DREAMS

MAJOR CAREER ACCOMPLISHMENTS

WHICH CAREER LADDERS YOU WANT TO CLIMB. MENTION SOME CAREER MILESTONES YOU WANT TO ACHIEVE.

AGE:

ACCOMPLISHMENT:

AGE:

ACCOMPLISHMENT:

AGE:

ACCOMPLISHMENT:

AGE:

ACCOMPLISHMENT:

AGE:

ACCOMPLISHMENT:

AGE:

ACCOMPLISHMENT:

AGE:

ACCOMPLISHMENT:

AGE:

ACCOMPLISHMENT:

AGE:

ACCOMPLISHMENT:

AGE:

ACCOMPLISHMENT:

AGE:

ACCOMPLISHMENT:

AGE:

ACCOMPLISHMENT:

GREATEST POSSIBLE THING YOU DESIRE:

WHY I DESIRE IT- CAREER

UNIVERSE BRINGS YOUR MANIFESTATIONS TO YOUR PHYSICAL TIMELINE MUCH FASTER IF YOU KNOW WHY EXACTLY YOU DESIRE WHAT YOU DESIRE. WRITE OUT WHY YOU WANT IT, WHERE YOU WANT TO UTILISE IT, ON WHOM YOU'RE GOING TO IMPLEMENT IT.
(DON'T FORGET YOURSELF & ALSO GIVING BACK TO OTHERS)

DAILY GRATITUDE JOURNAL

DATE:_____

MORNING GRATITUDE LOG:

EVENING GRATITUDE LOG:

PEOPLE I'M GRATEFUL FOR:
_____
_____
_____

THREE EXPERIENCES I'M GRATEFUL FOR:
_____
_____
_____

BEFORE BED GRATITUDE LOG:

THREE LESSONS LEARNT:

CAREER AFFIRMATIONS

1. My career is a journey, not a destination. I am in control of my career's journey.
2. I don't need the approval of others, because I believe in my goals and know what I am working toward.
3. I am capable of achieving my career goals, even when the journey isn't what I expected.
4. I don't have to know where I am going to have meaningful goals and to work with purpose.
5. I deserve to follow my passions and fight for the vision of my career.
6. I am passionate and dedicated to my career, even if I change my mind about my path.
7. I will fight against the systems holding myself and others back, because my voice matters.
8. I have the power to change directions, demand my worth, and push through challenges.
9. I am committed to creating my career on my terms.
10. I will use my voice and my power to lift up myself and those around me.

MANIFESTATION PLANNER

I DESIRE TO MANIFEST:

MY INTENTIONS BEHIND THE THINGS I WANT TO MANIFEST:

VISUALIZATION LOG:

5- STEP ACTION PLAN:

EVERY CHALLENGE I FACE IS AN OPPORTUNITY TO GROW AND IMPROVE. 11:11	I MOVE IN ALIGNMENT WITH MY HIGHEST SELF. 11:11
MY MIND IS CLEAR OF SELF-DOUBT, AND I AM READY TO EMBRACE EVERY CHALLENGE THAT COMES MY WAY. 11:11	I CAN POWERFULLY ATTRACT WHAT I WANT. 11:11
I AM WORTHY OF ACCOMPLISHMENT, SUCCESS, AND ABUNDANCE. 11:11	I MANIFEST MY FULL POTENTIAL TO BEING. 11:11
I AFFIRM MY ABILITY TO MERGE TIMELINES, AND REJOICE AS EVERYTHING COMES TO ME WITH EASE. 11:11	THE WORLD IS FILLED WITH ENDLESS OPPORTUNITIES FOR ME. 11:11

MANIFESTATIONS TRACKER

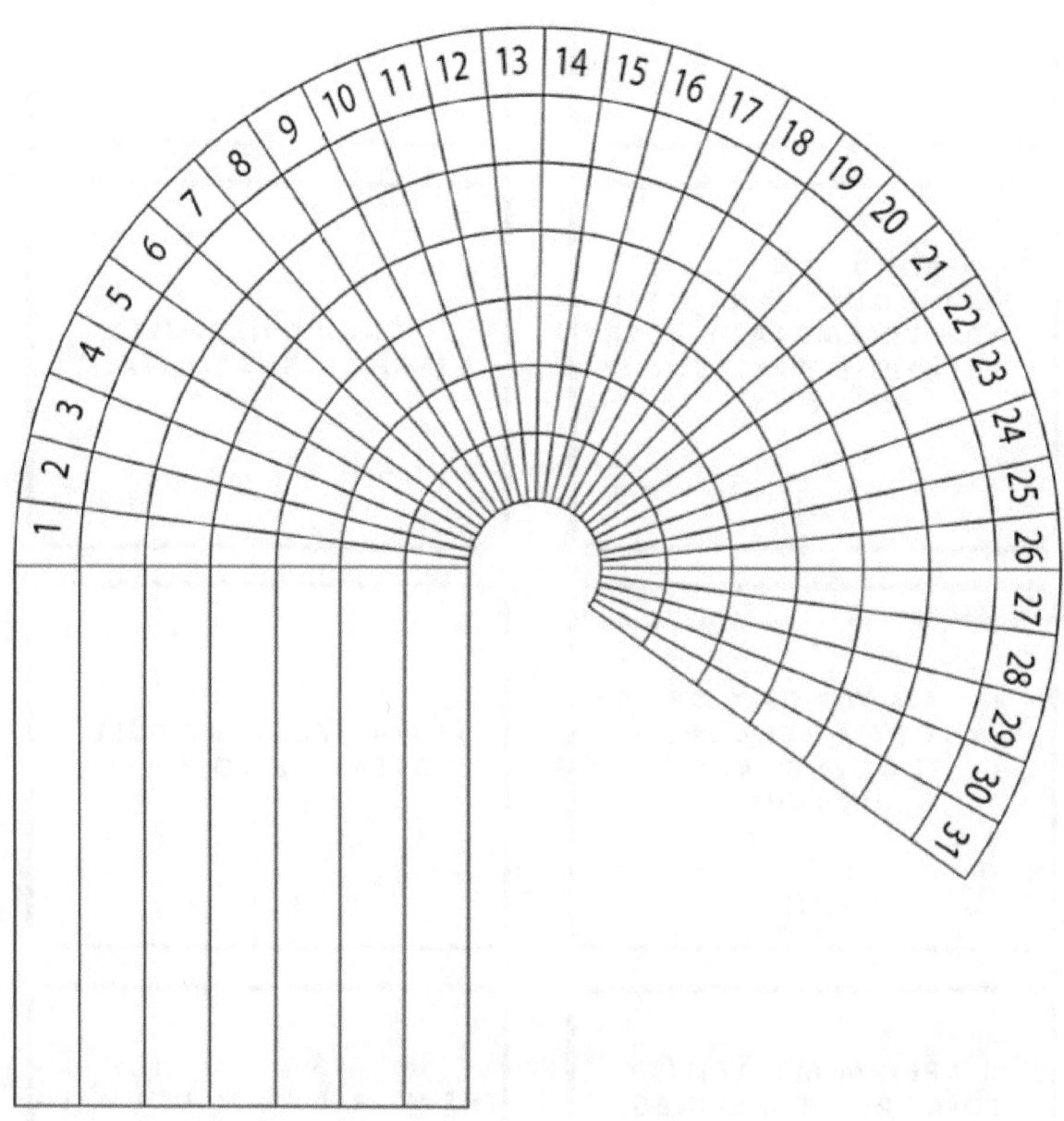

DAILY PLANNER

DATE:
DAY:

TODAY'S MANTRA:
_____

GRATEFUL FOR:
_____
_____
_____

WORK LIST:
_____
_____
_____
_____
_____

PERSONAL TO-DOS:

☐ _____
☐ _____
☐ _____
☐ _____

PRIORITY LIST:
_____
_____
_____

REMINDERS:
_____
_____

6:00 AM
6:30 AM
7:00 AM
7:30 AM
8:00 AM
8:30 AM
9:00 AM
9:30 AM
10:00 AM
10:30 AM
11:00 AM
11:30 AM
12:00 PM
12:30 PM
1:00 PM
1:30 PM
2:00 PM
2:30 PM
3:00 PM
3:30 PM
4:00 PM
4:30 PM
5:00 PM

GRATITUDE JAR
WRITE, DRAW OR ADD PICTURES OF THE THINGS YOU'RE GRATEFUL FOR

WEEKLY PLANNER

WEEK OF: _____

MONDAY	
TUESDAY	
WEDNESDAY	
THURSDAY	
FRIDAY	
SATURDAY	
SUNDAY	

IMPORTANT TASKS:

GOALS:

TO-DO LIST:

WEEKLY CALENDAR:

MON	TUE	WED	THU	FRI	SAT	SUN

A QUOTE TO LIVE BY: _____

ENERGY GOES WHERE INTENTIONS FLOWS.

I RECEIVED IT ALL & I FEEL

ASK THE UNIVERSE TO PROVIDE

THE 5-MINUTE JOURNAL

---ENDING THE DAY----

NAME :   DATE: /   /

GREAT THINGS THAT HAPPENED TODAY ...

_____
_____
_____
_____

THINGS I WISH WERE DIFFERENT...

_____
_____
_____
_____

THINGS I LEARNT / MY ACHIEVEMENTS...

_____
_____
_____
_____

THE 5-MINUTE JOURNAL

---ENDING THE DAY----

NAME :   DATE: /   /

GREAT THINGS THAT HAPPENED TODAY ...

_____

_____

_____

_____

THINGS I WISH WERE DIFFERENT...

_____

_____

_____

_____

THINGS I LEARNT / MY ACHIEVEMENTS...

_____

_____

_____

_____

THE 5-MINUTE JOURNAL

---ENDING THE DAY----

NAME :   DATE: /   /

GREAT THINGS THAT HAPPENED TODAY ...

_____
_____
_____
_____

THINGS I WISH WERE DIFFERENT...

_____
_____
_____
_____

THINGS I LEARNT / MY ACHIEVEMENTS...

_____
_____
_____
_____

THE 5-MINUTE JOURNAL

---ENDING THE DAY----

NAME : DATE: / /

GREAT THINGS THAT HAPPENED TODAY ...

_____
_____
_____
_____
_____

THINGS I WISH WERE DIFFERENT...

_____
_____
_____
_____
_____

THINGS I LEARNT / MY ACHIEVEMENTS...

_____
_____
_____
_____
_____

THE 5-MINUTE JOURNAL

---ENDING THE DAY---

NAME : DATE: / /

GREAT THINGS THAT HAPPENED TODAY ...

_____

_____

_____

_____

_____

THINGS I WISH WERE DIFFERENT...

_____

_____

_____

_____

THINGS I LEARNT / MY ACHIEVEMENTS...

_____

_____

_____

_____

_____

THE 5-MINUTE JOURNAL

---ENDING THE DAY----

NAME :   DATE: /   /

GREAT THINGS THAT HAPPENED TODAY ...

_____
_____
_____
_____
_____

THINGS I WISH WERE DIFFERENT...

_____
_____
_____
_____
_____

THINGS I LEARNT / MY ACHIEVEMENTS...

_____
_____
_____
_____
_____

THE 5-MINUTE JOURNAL

---ENDING THE DAY----

NAME :   DATE: /   /

GREAT THINGS THAT HAPPENED TODAY ...

_____
_____
_____
_____
_____

THINGS I WISH WERE DIFFERENT...

_____
_____
_____
_____

THINGS I LEARNT / MY ACHIEVEMENTS...

_____
_____
_____
_____
_____

THE 5-MINUTE JOURNAL

---ENDING THE DAY----

NAME :   DATE: /   /

GREAT THINGS THAT HAPPENED TODAY ...

_____
_____
_____
_____
_____

THINGS I WISH WERE DIFFERENT...

_____
_____
_____
_____
_____

THINGS I LEARNT / MY ACHIEVEMENTS...

_____
_____
_____
_____
_____

THE 5-MINUTE JOURNAL

---ENDING THE DAY----

NAME :   DATE: /   /

GREAT THINGS THAT HAPPENED TODAY ...

_____
_____
_____
_____

THINGS I WISH WERE DIFFERENT...

_____
_____
_____
_____

THINGS I LEARNT / MY ACHIEVEMENTS...

_____
_____
_____
_____

THE 5-MINUTE JOURNAL

---ENDING THE DAY----

NAME : DATE: / /

GREAT THINGS THAT HAPPENED TODAY ...

_____
_____
_____
_____

THINGS I WISH WERE DIFFERENT...

_____
_____
_____
_____

THINGS I LEARNT / MY ACHIEVEMENTS...

_____
_____
_____
_____

THE 5-MINUTE JOURNAL

---ENDING THE DAY----

NAME : DATE: / /

GREAT THINGS THAT HAPPENED TODAY ...

_____
_____
_____
_____

THINGS I WISH WERE DIFFERENT...

_____
_____
_____
_____

THINGS I LEARNT / MY ACHIEVEMENTS...

_____
_____
_____
_____

ANNUAL GOALS

FINANCE

INTENTION	BY	DONE

LOVE

INTENTION	BY	DONE

CAREER

INTENTION	BY	DONE

QUARTERLY GOALS

FINANCE

INTENTION	BY	DONE

LOVE

INTENTION	BY	DONE

CAREER

INTENTION	BY	DONE

PRAYERS

DATE	PRAYER	PRAYED

TWO-MONTHS GOALS

FINANCE

INTENTION	BY	DONE

LOVE

INTENTION	BY	DONE

CAREER

INTENTION	BY	DONE

THE 1 x 11 MANIFESTATION

THE 1×11 MANIFESTATION METHOD CONSISTS OF SETTING A CLEAR INTENTION AND THEN WRITING A SPECIFIC AFFIRMATION STATEMENT 11 TIMES IN THE MORNING, AND 11 TIMES IN THE EVENING BEFORE BED FOR 11 DAYS STRAIGHT.

NIGHT: DATE:_____

THE 55x5 MANIFESTATION

WRITE DOWN YOUR AFFIRMATION/WHAT YOU WANT TO MANIFEST FOR 55 TIMES FOR 5 DAYS IN A ROW

DAY: _____

BREATHE

THE 1 x 11 MANIFESTATION

THE 1×11 MANIFESTATION METHOD CONSISTS OF SETTING A CLEAR INTENTION AND THEN WRITING A SPECIFIC AFFIRMATION STATEMENT 11 TIMES IN THE MORNING, AND 11 TIMES IN THE EVENING BEFORE BED FOR 11 DAYS STRAIGHT.

MORNING: DATE:_____

THE 1 x 11 MANIFESTATION

THE 1×11 MANIFESTATION METHOD CONSISTS OF SETTING A CLEAR INTENTION AND THEN WRITING A SPECIFIC AFFIRMATION STATEMENT 11 TIMES IN THE MORNING, AND 11 TIMES IN THE EVENING BEFORE BED FOR 11 DAYS STRAIGHT.

EVENING: **DATE:** _____

I'm tuned into the flow of Prosperity.

THE 3-6-9 MANIFESTATION

6 AFTERNOON MANIFESTATIONS:

9 BEDTIME MANIFESTATIONS:

THE 3-6-9 MANIFESTATION

3 MORNING VISUALIZATIONS:

3 MORNING MANIFESTATIONS:

MORNING ENERGY CHECK:

TODAY'S MANTRA:

mindset is everything

MIRACLES LOG

DATE	THE MIRACLE	EFFECT ON ME

LIMITING BELIEFS: SOLUTION

WHAT LIMITING BELIEFS I HOLD	HOW TO GET RID OF THAT?
1.	
2.	
3.	
4.	
5.	
6.	
7.	
8.	
9.	
10.	
11.	
12.	
13.	
14.	
15.	
16.	
17.	
18.	
19.	
20.	
21.	
22.	
23.	

LIMITING BELIEFS: QUESTION

WHAT LIMITING BELIEFS I HOLD	WHY?
1.	
2.	
3.	
4.	
5.	
6.	
7.	
8.	
9.	
10.	
11.	
12.	
13.	
14.	
15.	
16.	
17.	
18.	
19.	
20.	
21.	
22.	
23.	

you're doing it right.

FAMILY VISION BOARD

WHY I DESIRE IT- FAMILY

UNIVERSE BRINGS YOUR MANIFESTATIONS TO YOUR PHYSICAL TIMELINE MUCH FASTER IF YOU KNOW WHY EXACTLY YOU DESIRE WHAT YOU DESIRE. WRITE OUT WHY YOU WANT IT, WHERE YOU WANT TO UTILISE IT, ON WHOM YOU'RE GOING TO IMPLEMENT IT.
(DON'T FORGET YOURSELF & ALSO GIVING BACK TO OTHERS)

LET'S VISUALIZE IT! -- FAMILY

PUT YOUR ROSE-COLOURED GLASSES ON, AND VISUALIZE EVERY ASPECT OF MONEY & WEALTH YOU DESIRE TO MANIFEST INTO YOUR PHYSICAL REALITY. THINK OF THE TINIEST DETAILS. TOUCH EVERY SENSE OF MONEY. WHAT IT MEANS TO YOU, HOW YOU FEEL ABOUT IT & EVERY LITTLE DETAIL! PUT NO BOUNDARIES TO YOUR DESIRES, LET YOUR IMAGINATION RUN FREE & WILD!

LET'S VISUALIZE IT! -- CAREER

PUT YOUR ROSE-COLOURED GLASSES ON, AND VISUALIZE EVERY ASPECT OF MONEY & WEALTH YOU DESIRE TO MANIFEST INTO YOUR PHYSICAL REALITY. THINK OF THE TINIEST DETAILS. TOUCH EVERY SENSE OF MONEY. WHAT IT MEANS TO YOU, HOW YOU FEEL ABOUT IT & EVERY LITTLE DETAIL! PUT NO BOUNDARIES TO YOUR DESIRES, LET YOUR IMAGINATION RUN FREE & WILD!

SELF-CARE VISION BOARD

BANK OF UNIVERSE

WRITE CHEQUES TO UNIVERSE: SPECIFY THE AMOUNT YOU WANT TO WITHDRAW FROM THE BANK OF UNIVERSE!

CHEQUE 8633
- YOUR NAME
- ADDRESS
- PURPOSE
- AMOUNT $
- 1335 6358 5321 813 _____ BANK

MONEY AFFIRMATIONS

1. Prosperity within me, prosperity around me.
2. Money is energy, so money is good.
3. I am abundant, rich, wealthy, deserving, worthy.
4. My life is full of wealth beyond money.
5. Money is in my mind. My mind creates money.
6. I will be healthy, wealthy, and happy.
7. I am happy, healthy, and wealthy.
8. I love money, and money loves me.
9. Money comes easily, frequently, and abundantly.
10. Every day, in every way, I am becoming richer and more prosperous.

MONEY VISION BOARD

WHY I DESIRE IT- MONEY

UNIVERSE BRINGS YOUR MANIFESTATIONS TO YOUR PHYSICAL TIMELINE MUCH FASTER IF YOU KNOW WHY EXACTLY YOU DESIRE WHAT YOU DESIRE. WRITE OUT WHY YOU WANT IT, WHERE YOU WANT TO UTILISE IT, ON WHOM YOU'RE GOING TO IMPLEMENT IT.
(DON'T FORGET YOURSELF & ALSO GIVING BACK TO OTHERS)

LET'S VISUALIZE IT! -- MONEY

PUT YOUR ROSE-COLOURED GLASSES ON, AND VISUALIZE EVERY ASPECT OF MONEY & WEALTH YOU DESIRE TO MANIFEST INTO YOUR PHYSICAL REALITY. THINK OF THE TINIEST DETAILS. TOUCH EVERY SENSE OF MONEY. WHAT IT MEANS TO YOU, HOW YOU FEEL ABOUT IT & EVERY LITTLE DETAIL! PUT NO BOUNDARIES TO YOUR DESIRES, LET YOUR IMAGINATION RUN FREE & WILD!

IT'S ALREADY YOURS!

— UNIVERSE

Let's Connect

Newsletter

Sign up for our monthly newsletter and receive up to date information on new products and information to assist and support you in your continued personal growth and so much more.
https://www.moreenjordan.com
and go to sign up for Newsletter

Social Media Facebook:

@AspiringLifeChange Counseling & Consulting

Website
https://www.moreenjordan.com

Wrapping Up!

Self care is extremely important. You can give more, and you can become more connected with yourself. You will be able to handle stress better and you can become more productive in your day and relationships. These are just a few of the benefits of effective self care. It is important to re-evaluation your self care levels and needs throughout your life. You can take the self care quiz whenever you feel there has been life changes and your need to re-evaluate if you are still addressing caring well for yourself

You can do this.
You deserve this!
Self care is not selfish!

www.ingramcontent.com/pod-product-compliance
Lightning Source LLC
Chambersburg PA
CBHW081420080526
44589CB00016B/2613